A TRUE BOOK™

The Most Endangered
Bears

KATIE MARSICO

Children's Press®
An Imprint of Scholastic Inc.

Content Consultant
Dr. Stephen S. Ditchkoff
Professor of Wildlife Sciences
Auburn University, Auburn, Alabama

Library of Congress Cataloging-in-Publication Data
Names: Marsico, Katie, 1980– author.
Title: Bears / by Katie Marsico.
Other titles: True book.
Description: New York, NY : Children's Press, an imprint of Scholastic Inc., 2017. | Series: A true
    book | Includes bibliographical references and index.
Identifiers: LCCN 2016025111| ISBN 9780531227251 (library binding) | ISBN
    9780531232767 (pbk.)
Subjects: LCSH: Bears—Conservation—Juvenile literature. |
    Pandas—Conservation—Juvenile literature. | Endangered species—Juvenile
    literature.
Classification: LCC QL737.C27 M3468 2017 | DDC 599.78—dc23
LC record available at https://lccn.loc.gov/2016025111

© 2017 Scholastic Inc.
All rights reserved. Published in 2017 by Children's Press, an imprint of Scholastic Inc.
Printed in China 62
SCHOLASTIC, CHILDREN'S PRESS, A TRUE BOOK™, and associated logos are trademarks and/or
registered trademarks of Scholastic Inc.
1 2 3 4 5 6 7 8 9 10 R 26 25 24 23 22 21 20 19 18 17

Front cover: Polar bear mother and cubs
Back cover: Giant panda mother and cubs

Find the Truth!

Everything you are about to read is true *except* for one of the sentences on this page.

Which one is **TRUE**?

T or F   Six bear species are officially vulnerable.

T or F   About 2,000 polar bears exist in the wild.

Find the answers in this book.

Contents

THE **BIG** TRUTH!

The Food Chain

A polar bear

A brown bear
mother and cub

4 A Chance to Change the Story

How are conservationists
working to save bears?..................... **33**

A sun bear

Keeping Bears Safe

How many pandas do you see in the photo on page 6? If you answered four, guess again! Only the little one is a panda. The others are staff members at the China **Conservation** and Research Center for the Giant Panda (CCRCGP). The CCRCGP is located at the Wolong National Nature Reserve in China's Sichuan province. Staff members wear these outfits while providing medical care to panda cubs born at the center.

⬅ As of 2016, the CCRCGP has raised and released six pandas.

The less human contact a panda has at the CCRCGP, the more likely it is the panda will survive in the wild.

Here to Help

CCRCGP workers dress up to make medical examinations less stressful for their panda patients. They also want to limit the amount of time the cubs spend with humans. Ultimately, the CCRCGP tries to release certain pandas into their natural habitats. This is harder to accomplish if the bears grow too accustomed to being around people. By wearing costumes, staff members prepare pandas to survive independently in the wild.

A caregiver checks the health of a newborn giant panda at the Wolong National Nature Reserve.

The CCRCGP focuses on panda research and conservation. Their efforts include a captive **breeding** program. By releasing cubs born in captivity, conservationists hope to help pandas avoid **extinction**.

Fewer than 2,000 pandas exist in the wild. As a result of habitat loss, they are vulnerable, or at risk of becoming extinct. Pandas are just one of several bear species facing an uncertain future.

Big Trouble for Bears

Bears are large **mammals** found throughout North America, South America, Europe, and Asia. There are eight bear species: Asiatic black bears, brown bears, American black bears, giant pandas, polar bears, sloth bears, spectacled bears, and sun bears. Asiatic black bears, giant pandas, polar bears, sloth bears, spectacled bears, and sun bears are considered vulnerable.

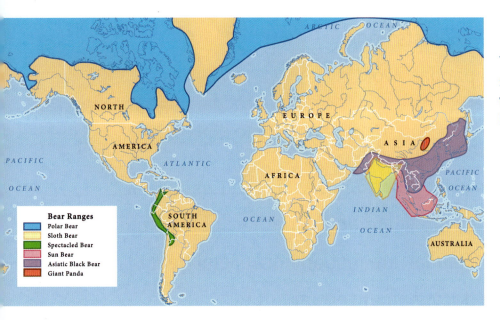

This map shows where vulnerable bears live in the wild.

Bear Ranges
- Polar Bear
- Sloth Bear
- Spectacled Bear
- Sun Bear
- Asiatic Black Bear
- Giant Panda

Warmer summers
and shrinking polar ice caps
cause problems for polar bears.

Pandas were once considered endangered, which means they had an even higher risk of disappearing. In September 2016, their status changed to vulnerable. Even so, there are few guarantees these and other vulnerable bears will survive without help.

Human activity has taken a toll on these majestic mammals. Habitat loss, climate change, **poaching**, and the **exotic** pet trade all threaten their future.

CHAPTER 2

Majestic Mammals

Bears live in a wide variety of habitats. Many species make their homes in forests. Others are found in desert regions, throughout grasslands, or on or along Arctic sea ice.

Most bears spend some of their time in dens, or hidden lairs. They often construct these resting spots in hollow trees, caves, snowbanks, and narrow rock openings. Bears may also dig dens in hillsides or amid clumps of bushes and shrubs.

Female brown bears give birth only once every three years.

From Littlest to Largest

Bear sizes, habitats, and eating habits vary a great deal among different species.

A COMPARISON OF BEAR SPECIES

Photograph	Species	Weight (Adults)	Habitat	Diet
	American black bear	88 to 496 pounds (40 to 225 kg)	Coniferous (evergreen) and deciduous (sheds leaves in fall) forests	Roots, buds, berries, nuts, fruits, and honey; sometimes small mammals and caribou
	Asiatic black bear	110 to 440 pounds (50 to 199.6 kg)	Coniferous and deciduous forests	Acorns, nuts, fruits, and berries; sometimes insects and small mammals
	Brown bear	441 to 1,500 pounds (200 to 680.4 kg)	Deciduous forests	Grasses, fruits, nuts, honey, insects, mammals, and fish
	Giant panda	220 to 330 pounds (99.8 to 149.7 kg)	Deciduous and mixed forests	Almost exclusively bamboo
	Polar bear	776 to 1,500 pounds (352 to 680.4 kg)	On or along sea ice	Primarily seals
	Sloth bear	120 to 310 pounds (54.4 to 140.6 kg)	Forests and grasslands	Insects, fruits, flowers, and honey
	Spectacled bear	309 to 386 pounds (140 to 175 kg)	Cloud forests and mountainous grasslands	Fruits, tree bark, bulbs and other plant parts, insects, small rodents, and birds
	Sun bear	77 to 176 pounds (35 to 79.8 kg)	Tropical forests	Fruits, insects, birds, and small rodents

Shape, Movement, and Speed

As different as bear species are, they share certain physical traits. For starters, they all have a stocky body, short tail, and four sturdy legs. Each of their paws features five toes and thick, powerful claws.

Bears are able to move short distances on just their hind limbs. For the most part, however, they walk and run on all fours. Some bears reach speeds of up to 40 miles (64 kilometers) per hour.

A sun bear's strong paws and sharp claws help make it an excellent tree climber.

Polar bears have an extremely thin layer of skin that covers their eyes and helps them see underwater.

Eyes, Ears, and Nose

Most bears have small eyes and likely do not see things well from a distance. They mainly rely on the nose at the end of their long snout to track down prey. In fact, some bears have been known to sniff out food that's up to 20 miles (32 km) away! The size and shape of their ears vary, depending on the specific species. And their hearing is twice as good as humans.

Dental Features and Diet

Bears are generally opportunistic—they devour whatever food is available. Most bears have 42 teeth, though sloth bears have 40. A bear's long, pointed canine teeth can grasp prey. It uses its short, sharp teeth at the front, called incisors, to snip off bits of plant or meat. Flatter, wider premolars and molars at the back crush the bear's food before it's swallowed.

A bear's teeth are shaped for different tasks.

Incisors

Canine teeth

Premolars and molars

Waiting for Warmer Weather

Apart from pandas, most bears undergo some form of **hibernation**. When food becomes harder to find during colder weather, they move into a den. Once inside, a bear's temperature drops, and its breathing, heart rate, and **metabolism** slow down. During this period, the bear is less active and requires less energy, so it doesn't need to feed as frequently. Some bears hibernate for more than 100 days without eating, drinking, or going to the bathroom!

A black bear mother and cub rest in their den during the winter.

Fabulous Fur

Different bears have different colored fur. Depending on the species, fur can be black, brown, white, or a mix of these colors. Some species, such as pandas and spectacled bears, are known for their unique markings. Lighter coloring around a spectacled bear's eyes resembles spectacles, or glasses.

Fur protects bears against heat and cold. It also allows them to blend in with their surroundings. This helps bears avoid being spotted by their enemies.

The markings on a spectacled bear's face make it easy to recognize.

Animal Enemies

Adult bears generally have a limited number of natural predators. Wolves and certain big cats are occasionally a threat to cubs. It's also not unusual for adult male bears, called boars, to pose a danger to each other and to cubs. Fighting for power, food and water, or a mate sometimes leads to serious injuries or even death. Overall, however, the biggest problems bears face involve human activity.

Two polar bears fight in Alaska.

Regional Risks

The brown bear is one of the most wide-ranging land mammals in the world. It is found across northern Europe, Asia, and northwestern North America. However, this is much smaller than its original range. South of Canada, its North American home is just 2 percent what it once was. These bears once extended south to central Mexico, and west into Missouri. Now, they're limited to northwestern Montana, the northwest tip of Washington, and Yellowstone National Park.

A Little About Life Cycle

Depending on the species, bears have been known to survive for up to 40 years in the wild. For most of that period, they prefer to live alone. Bears generally only come together to reproduce, or produce young. Adult females, or sows, typically have one to three cubs at a time. Baby bears remain with their mother between one and three years.

A sow watches over her two young cubs.

A brown bear rubs its back against a tree.

Bear Talk

Bears use noises such as cries, roars, purrs, and growls to communicate. They also rely on posture, movement, and even odor. For example, scientists have observed bears rubbing against tree bark. The smell they leave behind probably helps them attract mates. It is one of many features of bear behavior that scientists are eager to learn more about!

The Food Chain

Polar bears are apex predators—they sit atop the food chain in their Arctic **ecosystem**. So, when their population numbers change, the effect ripples downward. Let's take a look at how it works.

POLAR BEARS

Polar bears are powerful swimmers and fierce hunters. Ringed seals make up a large part of a polar bear's diet. As a result, fewer polar bears would probably mean more ringed seals.

RINGED SEALS

Ringed seals live in ice-covered areas throughout the Arctic seas. They feed on fish such as Arctic cod. If ringed seal populations rose, more Arctic cod would probably be eaten, reducing the fish's population.

ARCTIC COD

Arctic cod are small fish found in Arctic waters. They feed mostly on tiny crustaceans, or shelled sea creatures, called copepods. If there were fewer Arctic cod, the copepod population would likely rise.

COPEPODS

Copepods are tiny creatures related to crayfish and water fleas. Diatoms, a simple **alga**, form the bulk of a copepod's diet. A higher copepod population could lead to more diatoms being consumed, leaving fewer diatoms.

DIATOMS

Diatoms use light to produce their own food in a process called photosynthesis. Photosynthesis releases oxygen, which almost all living things—including people— need to survive. In addition, diatoms are at the base of many other food chains. Changes in their population affect the living things connected to these food chains.

A black bear reaches for huckleberries high in a tree.

CHAPTER 3

Under Threat

Bear conservation isn't just about saving bears. These mammals frequently sit at the top of the food chain. Their survival impacts the health of their entire ecosystem.

Many bear species also support plant growth as well. After feeding on plants, bears produce waste that contains the plants' seeds. This process helps new plants develop throughout the various environments where bears exist.

← Bears sometimes climb trees to reach high-growing fruits and berries.

Areas that were once forest are left cleared by deforestation in Laos, a country in Southeast Asia.

Losing Living Space

Conservationists recognize the need to protect bears. But it's tough. People continue to clear forests and other natural habitats for logging, farming, building, and transportation projects. These activities limit where pandas, sun bears, sloth bears, spectacled bears, and Asiatic black bears can feed and reproduce. Habitat destruction also forces bears into areas where people live and work. This creates potentially dangerous situations for both bears and humans.

A Frozen World That's Fading Away

Habitat loss threatens polar bears as well. People drill for oil in the Arctic, where polar bears live. They use the oil to heat homes, fuel cars, and other uses. Drilling also leads to noise and oil spills. Both negatively impact local wildlife.

Climate change is another threat. Pollution adds harmful substances to the atmosphere, causing the atmosphere to hold in more of the sun's heat. Temperatures rise and sea ice melts more quickly. In turn, the polar bear's frozen world gradually disappears.

An oil platform drills for oil in the Arctic Ocean.

Polar bear hunting in Alaska is controlled. Native Americans who live in the state are allowed to hunt these bears, but it is illegal for anyone else to do it.

Polar bear hides

Illegal Hunting

Poaching is another big problem facing bear species. For most of these bears, hunting is not the main cause of their vulnerability. However, illegal hunting can bring species that are already at risk into even greater danger. Some poachers hunt bears for their meat or fur. Others pursue these animals mainly for sport or for their body parts. In traditional medicine, bear paws and organs like gallbladders are used to treat everything from fevers to heart disease.

Trapped in the Pet Trade

The exotic pet trade is also a huge threat to bears. People involved in this business frequently separate cubs from their mothers to sell them. But caring for a wild animal isn't easy. Bears trapped in the pet trade often suffer from poor nutrition and are housed in cramped cages. As they grow larger, they sometimes become dangerous to handle. Many of these bears end up abandoned, abused, ill, or dead.

Bears are cute when they are cubs, but they grow up to be powerful and dangerous animals.

A veterinarian helps a rescued bear cub munch on a piece of fruit.

CHAPTER 4

A Chance to Change the Story

Conservationists work hard to save bears in a variety of ways. One involves creating protected areas such as national parks, preserves, and **sanctuaries**. Typically, hunting is limited or completely restricted within these locations. So is land development that would change or destroy the natural landscape.

Bear conservation also includes replanting trees and grasses. This helps restore bears' wild habitats. It provides various species with additional space to feed and reproduce.

Brown bears are often victims of illegal smuggling around the world.

A park ranger answers questions from park visitors.

Making People More Aware

For conservation to work, the public needs to understand the threats that bears face. Activities, speeches, and other programs at schools, nature centers, and zoos help accomplish this goal. There are also outreach efforts aimed at hunters, farmers, and land developers. Ultimately, both humans and wildlife will suffer if any of the eight bear species disappear.

Protectors' Roles

Wildlife biologists and park rangers are essential to bear conservation. These men and women often monitor different bear populations. They also remain on the lookout for signs of illegal hunting or any activity that poses a threat to wildlife. Rangers act as educators, too. They provide visitors with information about local bear species, as well as safety tips. The knowledge these experts share helps people both respect nature and avoid bear attacks.

Providing Legal Protection

Many conservationists focus on reaching out to lawmakers. In some areas, it is illegal to hunt or disturb vulnerable bear species. Yet laws aren't successful without proper enforcement.

Conservationists also coordinate international legal efforts. This is important because the exotic animal trade occurs around the world. The sale of medicines and souvenirs linked to illegal hunting is also international.

A Peek Into the Giant Panda's Past

600,000 years ago
The earliest giant pandas appear.

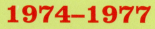

Early 1960s
People set up the earliest panda preserves.

1974–1977
Studies reveal that only 2,459 pandas exist in the wild.

Scientific Studies

Scientific research plays a major role in bear conservation. Many scientists try to learn more about bears in the wild. Sometimes they attach electronic tracking devices to the animals they're observing. This provides information about a bear's behavior and life cycle. In other situations, researchers study bears in captivity. Some of these scientists also oversee captive breeding programs.

1983

A wildlife protection law increases panda conservation.

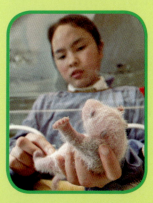

2014

Scientists estimate there are just under 2,000 wild pandas left in the wild.

September 2016

Officials announce that the panda's status has changed from endangered to vulnerable.

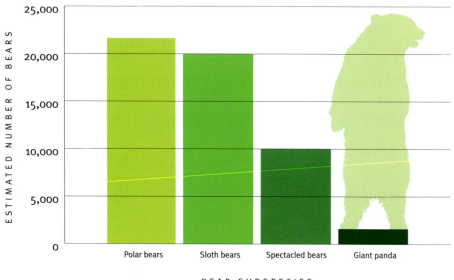

Bear Subspecies Populations

ESTIMATED NUMBER OF BEARS

25,000

20,000

15,000

10,000

5,000

0

Polar bears　　Sloth bears　　Spectacled bears　　Giant panda

BEAR SUBSPECIES

Keeping Track

Researchers also study bears in the wild to estimate how many members of a species remain. Radio and satellite tracking often form parts of these studies. People also try to observe these animals in person. Experts estimate between 22,000 and 31,000 polar bears live in the wild. This number is likely less than 20,000 for sloth bears. For spectacled bears, it's probably no more than 10,000.

Scientists are confident that Asiatic black bears and sun bears have decreased in number. Yet they struggle to reliably estimate how many remain. There are probably more Asiatic black bears and sun bears, however, than giant pandas. With a population of about 2,000 animals, pandas are the rarest of all bear species.

There is no way to foresee the future, but there is hope for bears if people take action in the present. ★

Scientists still have a lot to learn about sun bears, from their habits to the size of their population.

CALLING ALL CONSERVATIONISTS!

Conservationists represent all walks of life. Some are scientists. Others are kids just like you! What can you do to help? Here are a few ideas to get you started.

DONATION

RAISE AWARENESS

Bear Awareness Week is the third week in May. Get creative. Making posters and collages of vulnerable bears to hang at school is one idea. Another possibility is sharing a few short facts about bear conservation during school announcements. Talk to your student council and principal.

"ADOPT" A BEAR

For a fee, some zoos and conservation groups allow people to "adopt" a wild animal. You won't actually end up with a giant panda or polar bear in your home. But you'll probably receive photos of your animal, information on its history, and updates on how it's doing. Ask a trusted adult for help.

PROTECT THE ENVIRONMENT

Our everyday decisions impact the environment. Sit down with your family and figure out five simple steps you'll take together to save bears. For example, try walking more and using the car less. This helps reduce gases that contribute to pollution and climate change.

INVITE AN EXPERT

Contact bear conservation organizations with the help of an adult. Find out if they ever send guest speakers to schools. Alternately, ask if they'd be willing to conduct an interview with your class via Skype or e-mail. Be sure to talk to your teacher before you make any arrangements!

Conservation Vs. the Energy Crisis

Alaska's Arctic National Wildlife Refuge (ANWR) is the United States' largest protected wilderness area. It is home to many species, including polar bears and brown bears. The region is also rich in oil and natural gas. Some people want to change laws to allow drilling for oil and gas there. Others worry such operations will cause too much damage to the land and local wildlife.

Which side do you agree with? Why?

Yes Allow drilling!

It's important to respect natural habitats within the ANWR. But there are ways to practice conservation and still address the growing energy

crisis. Earth contains limited supplies of oil and natural gas. People rely on these resources for energy. **Without drilling in new areas, the prices of oil and gas will skyrocket.** This will impact everything from financial markets to international relations. Plus, drilling doesn't have to be allowed everywhere in the ANWR. People should figure out how to protect their own long-term needs and those of wildlife.

No Protect natural habitats!

The ANWR supports 45 species of mammals, 42 species of fish, and more than 200 species of migratory birds. (Migratory animals move from place to place at certain times of year.) **The machinery used to drill for gas and oil creates noise that can injure or confuse animals in the water. There is also the risk of oil spills, which damage water, land, and wildlife.** These practices will destroy natural areas that wildlife depend on to feed and reproduce. It's likely that such changes will drive some animals—including polar bears—even closer to extinction. It's true that not every part of the ANWR would necessarily have to be opened up to drilling. However, will people ever know for certain how much is too much? What amount of habitat destruction will push certain species over the edge? Let's not drill in the Arctic!

True Statistics

Number of giant pandas that exist in the wild: About 2,000

Number of bear species that are endangered: 1

Number of bear species that are vulnerable: 5

Minimum weight of most adult sun bears: 77 lbs. (35 kg)

Maximum weight of most adult polar bears: 1,500 lbs. (680.4 kg)

Number of teeth most bear species have: 42

Number of days some bears can go without eating, drinking, or going to the bathroom (during hibernation): More than 100

Length of time some bears have been known to live in the wild: Up to 40 years

Number of years cubs remain with their mother after birth: 1 to 3

Did you find the truth?

T Six bear species are officially vulnerable.

F Only about 2,000 polar bears exist in the wild.

Resources

Books

Claus, Matteson. *Animals and Deforestation*. New York: Gareth Stevens Publishing, 2014.

Shea, Nicole. *Poaching and Illegal Trade*. New York: Gareth Stevens Publishing, 2014.

Stefoff, Rebecca. *Polar Bears*. New York: Cavendish Square, 2016.

Zeiger, Jennifer. *Pandas*. New York: Children's Press, 2012.

Important Words

alga (AL-juh) a small plant without roots or stems that grows mainly in water

breeding (BREE-ding) keeping animals or plants under controlled conditions so they reproduce more and healthier offspring

conservation (kahn-sur-VAY-shuhn) the protection of valuable things, especially forests, wildlife, natural resources, or artistic or historic objects

ecosystem (EE-koh-sis-tuhm) all the living things in a particular area

exotic (ig-ZAH-tik) from a faraway country

extinction (ik-STINGKT-shuhn) the permanent disappearance of a living thing

hibernation (hye-bur-NAY-shuhn) sleeping through the entire winter in order to survive when temperatures are cold and food is hard to find

mammals (MAM-uhlz) warm-blooded animals that have hair or fur and usually give birth to live babies; female mammals produce milk to feed their young

metabolism (muh-TAB-uh-liz-uhm) the process in the body that changes the food one eats into the energy needed to breathe, digest, and grow

poaching (POH-ching) hunting or fishing illegally

sanctuaries (SANGK-choo-er-eez) natural areas where birds or animals are protected from hunters

Index

Page numbers in **bold** indicate illustrations.

About the Author

Katie Marsico graduated from Northwestern University and worked as an editor in reference publishing before she began writing in 2006. Since that time, she has published more than 200 titles for children and young adults. Ms. Marsico loves polar bears, though she'd never want to get too close to one!